BABOUSHKA

CHARACTERS:
Storyteller, Baboushka, Nadya, Boris, Zlotta, Stefan, Alexa, Tammo, Ivan, Nicko, First King, Second King, Third King, Mary, Joseph, Children, Choir, Angel(s).

SCENE:
Baboushka is based on an ancient Russian legend. The action takes place mostly inside Baboushka's cottage, but some occurs in the snowy forest outside. There is a also a stable scene.

Retold by Moira Andrew
Illustrated by Holly Swain

Collins Educational
An Imprint of HarperCollinsPublishers

STORYTELLER: This is the story of Baboushka. It comes from an old Russian legend and takes place one winter's night in a dark forest, deep in the heart of Russia. Baboushka lives alone in her cottage in the forest.

Enter Baboushka pulling a sledge with logs on it.

BABOUSHKA: These logs are heavy, but I'm lucky to have found them. What a good fire I can build on this cold winter's night!

She takes some logs into the house and puts them on the fire.

That's better!

She holds her hands to the heat. She sings softly to herself as she puts cakes, wine and some glasses on the table.

Now everything is ready for the party!

Voices off. A knock at the door. Baboushka opens the door. Nadya, Boris, Stefan, Alexa and Zlotta enter one by one, taking off scarves and hats and brushing snow from their clothes.

BABOUSHKA: Come in, Nadya, come in. You must be frozen after your journey. Come in and sit by the fire.

NADYA: Good evening, Baboushka. It's good to see you again.
They hug one another.

BABOUSHKA: Come in all of you!
Boris, Stefan, Alexa and Zlotta each hug Baboushka in turn and look around her cottage.

BORIS: What a lovely cottage, Baboushka.

ZLOTTA: And so warm and cosy!

STEFAN: What's that delicious smell? *He sniffs.*

BABOUSHKA: I've baked some cakes for the party. *She hands them round.*

NADYA: Mmm, you do make delicious cakes, Baboushka.

BABOUSHKA: Boris, please pour the wine. *He does so. They all sip.* Do you like it? I made it from blackberries I found in the forest.

STEFAN: The wine tastes of summer. *He puts the glass on the table next to the window.* Did you notice the stars look extra bright tonight?

BABOUSHKA: The villagers were talking of nothing else.

ZLOTTA: No wonder they're excited. I've never seen stars shine like this before. Look everyone! *They all move to the window.*

ALEXA: With all the snow on the trees, the forest looks really beautiful. *They look out at the night. [Choir sings 'In the Bleak Midwinter'.]*

BABOUSHKA: *She turns from the window.* How I enjoy having my friends around me. Sometimes the forest can be so lonely, especially in winter. *She brightens up.* But it's not a night for sadness. More wine? Nadya?

NADYA: Just a drop, please. What a wonderful party! *All clink glasses.*

ZLOTTA: You are giving us an evening to remember, Baboushka!

They move back to sit around the fire. [Choir sings 'While Shepherds Watched'.] Then there is a knock at the door.

BABOUSHKA: Who can this be so late? *She opens the door.* Tammo, Ivan, Nicko! My shepherd friends. Come in and join us.

The three shepherds enter. They look very excited.

BORIS: What are you doing here, so far from your flock?

STEFAN: The night is cold and the wolves get hungry. Aren't you afraid for the sheep?

TAMMO: Yes, we are afraid. But something wonderful has happened…

IVAN: Something you simply won't believe!

All Baboushka's guests look interested.

BORIS: Then tell us, please tell us. Come and warm yourselves by the fire, and tell us what has happened.

TAMMO: It happened like this. We were fast asleep…

IVAN: …And we heard a voice…

NICKO: …A voice from heaven! The voice of an angel!

BABOUSHKA: An angel. What did he say?

TAMMO: He told us we should follow the brightest star in the sky…

IVAN: …And that this star would lead us to a stable…

NICKO: …And to a manger, like a cradle, with a newborn baby in it!

Alexa: A newborn baby in a manger! How strange!

Tammo: So we left our sheep to follow the star.

Ivan: Then we saw the light in your window, Baboushka.

Nicko: So we thought we'd like to tell you and perhaps warm ourselves by the fire.

Tammo: But now we must be on our way again. Will you come with us, Baboushka? Wouldn't you like to find this child?

Baboushka: I'm sorry, Tammo. I can't. As you see I have all my friends here. We're having a party! But, tell me, what's so special about this baby?

Ivan: We don't know exactly, but the angel said that he's a very special baby indeed. His name is Jesus.

Nicko: Won't you come with us, Baboushka?

Baboushka: No, I can't. How could I leave my friends?

Tammo: Then we must say goodbye. Thank you for the rest and food. We must follow the star.

The shepherds wrap their cloaks around them and go.

All: Goodbye!

Baboushka: Go carefully! Have a safe journey!
She turns from the door and shivers. I feel sad to see them go.

Storyteller: The hours pass quickly while they all chatter.

Boris: It's getting late. We must be going, Baboushka.

Zlotta: Thank you for the party.

Nadya: It's been a lovely evening. Goodbye and thank you.

Alexa: Take care of yourself, Baboushka.

STEFAN: Don't keep the door open. It's so cold outside. Goodbye Baboushka!

ALL: Goodbye and thank you!

The friends disappear into the night. Baboushka begins to clear the table, moving slowly. From time to time she looks out of the window.

BABOUSHKA: It's still snowing. I feel lonely now my friends have gone.

She sighs and sits by the dying fire holding her hands to the last of the heat. [Choir sings first verse of 'We Three Kings'.] The First King appears outside the cottage. He looks tired and cold.

FIRST KING: At last, a light! Perhaps someone will give me shelter.

When he reaches the door, he knocks. Baboushka looks out of the window. Then she opens the door just a crack.

BABOUSHKA: Who is knocking at my door so late at night?

First King: Good evening, my lady. Do not be afraid. I have travelled from lands far beyond the forest. Please may I rest? I am very weary.

Baboushka: Good evening, sir. Please come in. Why have you travelled so far on such a cold night? *The king enters.*

First King: Have you seen how bright the stars are tonight?

Baboushka: Yes, everyone is talking about it.

First King: My wise men have told me to follow the brightest star of all. They tell me it will lead to the new baby king. Will you come with me, my lady?

Baboushka: It is kind of you to ask, sir, but I can't. I have had friends in all evening so I must tidy my house. Will you have a cake and a glass of wine before you go, sir? *She passes him some cake and a glass of wine. He eats.*

First King: Thank you for your kindness, my lady. Now I must be on my way. Farewell! *He goes out.*

[*Choir sings the second verse of 'We Three Kings'.*] *Baboushka fusses about dusting. Then there is another knock at the door.*

BABOUSHKA: *Wearily.* Who is it this time? *She opens the door.*

SECOND KING: Good evening, my lady. I have travelled many miles and I am very tired. May I rest a while?

BABOUSHKA: Good evening, sir. Please come in. Why have you travelled so far on such a cold night? *The king enters.*

SECOND KING: I am following the brightest star in the sky. I am told it will lead me to the Christchild. Look, I have brought him a gift. Would you like to come with me, my lady?

BABOUSHKA: I'd like to come, of course, but I have no present for the baby. Will you have a cake and a glass of wine before you go, sir? *She passes him some cake and a glass of wine. He eats.*

SECOND KING: Thank you for your kindness, my lady. Now I must be on my way. Farewell! *He goes out.*

Baboushka: What a busy time I have had tonight with all these visitors. I must sit down and rest.

Baboushka sighs, then sits resting her head in her hands. [Choir sings another verse of 'We Three Kings'.] There is another knock at the door.

Baboushka: *Very wearily.* What now? *She gets up and opens the door.*

Third King: Good evening, my lady. May I come in and rest? I have travelled for many long days and nights.

Baboushka: Good evening, sir. Please come in. Why have you travelled so far on such a cold night? *The king enters.*

Third King: I have travelled far from the hot, sunny lands I know. I'm not used to all this ice and snow, but I have promised to follow the brightest star in the sky.

Baboushka: Lots of people have told me about this star. How did you find out so much about it, sir?

THIRD KING: My wise men study the stars. They say this one will lead to a baby king. Would you like to come with me, my lady?

BABOUSHKA: I'm becoming very curious about this baby. *She hesitates.* I'd like to come with you, but I can't. *She yawns.* I've been so busy today and now I really must rest. Will you have a cake and a glass of wine before you go, sir? *She passes him some cake and a glass of wine. He eats.*

THIRD KING: Thank you for your kindness, my lady. Now I must go. I must follow the star. Farewell! *He goes out and Baboushka sits down.*

BABOUSHKA: Now that everyone has gone and I am alone, it feels very quiet and cold. *She shivers and pulls her shawl around her shoulders.* I feel so sad and lonely.

She rocks herself to sleep in her chair. [The choir sings 'Away in a Manger', but Baboushka does nor stir.] The stable tableau is lit, showing Mary, Joseph and the angel(s) around the manger. When the carol ends, the lights fade. The shepherds and the kings meet in the forest. The kings are studying charts and reading the stars.

Tammo: Good evening, sirs. What brings you to the bitter snow and ice of this distant corner of the world?

First King: We have journeyed for many months over the mountains and across the seas. We have studied charts and stars.

Second King: Our charts have brought us to this icy place.

Third King: We have been told to follow the brightest star in the sky.

Ivan: *Very excited.* The star! That must be the star we are following, too!

First King: Then let us travel together.
The kings and shepherds travel towards the stable. [The choir sings 'Gloria in Excelsis Deo'.] Lights shine on the stable scene.

Storyteller: So the shepherds and kings set off together. They come at last to the stable and find Mary, Joseph and the baby Jesus. The shepherds bring a woollen coat for the baby and the kings offer rich gifts of gold and myrrh and frankincense. Then they kneel down to worship the baby.

The stable scene is mimed while the storyteller speaks. All the time, in the background, Baboushka sits sleeping by the ashes of her fire. [The choir sings 'O Little Town of Bethlehem'.]

STORYTELLER: After giving their gifts, the shepherds and kings part and go on their way. Meanwhile, Joseph is warned in a dream that King Herod plans to kill all the baby boys to make sure none can ever succeed to his crown. So Joseph takes Mary and the baby Jesus away to the safety of another country… and what of Baboushka?

BABOUSHKA: *She wakes and stretches.* That's better, I feel quite rested. But I do wish I had gone with the kings and shepherds to see the special baby. Why did I refuse? *She looks out of the window.* If I had a gift for him I'd go right now. Perhaps I could find something he'd like in the forest.

She pulls her shawl around her and goes out into the forest, closing the door behind her. She searches among the trees and on the ground but finds nothing.

BABOUSHKA: Nothing! I have nothing to give the baby. I am so sad. *She sobs, hands over her face.*

STORYTELLER: But there, where Baboushka's tears fall on the forest floor, she finds a pure, white rose.

Baboushka finds a Christmas rose and holds it up.

BABOUSHKA: A rose! In winter, too! It must be meant for the Christchild. I'll take it as my gift and go to search for the baby. I hope I'm not too late.

STORYTELLER: But Baboushka is too late. Every person, every star and every sign has gone by the time she reaches the stable. *Mime of Baboushka arriving at the empty stable, sadly leaving her gift of a single white rose. She leaves the stable.* She searches and searches as the days stretch into weeks, the weeks into months, and the months into years.

Children arrive and sit playing in the stable. Baboushka takes little brightly wrapped gifts from her basket and gives one to each of the children.

STORYTELLER: And the legend says that Baboushka is searching still. Every Christmas she makes up little gifts and gives them to all the babies and young children she can find in the forlorn hope that one day she will find the Christchild.

[Choir sings 'Silent Night' as all the players group themselves round Baboushka and the children.]